52
Weeks for Me
Self Care

Nina B

The 52 Week Experience Journal Series ©

All rights reserved. No parts of this book may be copied or reproduced for any reason in any form without written permission from the author.

Opal Raye Publications

www.the52weekexperience.com

The52weekexperience@yahoo.com

443.567.8886

Note to self…

I will never lose you again….

Before you start this 52 week journey, leave yourself notes, mantras, words of affirmation or whatever gives you peace and positive energy below to take along the way…

Congratulations on making time for YOU!

Reconnect with life and all the good things that it actually has to offer YOU.

Children, jobs/careers/businesses, marriage/relationships, bad dating and more can take so much from us… After you have given everything to everyone else- What's left for you???

Why wait on anyone to make plans with or for you when you can do things for you. In this edition you have 52 weeks of activities and tools to do with and for self. And if you choose a few activities you can include friends in on too!

Place new experiences in your memory bank and use the spaces here to pen the positive along the way. This serves as a good keepsake to look back on the great times had as you reconnect with self…

Your heart will thank you.

Example of how to journal your journey:

- ❖ **Spa Day**
  - ➢ Date: November 11 2011
  - ➢ Spa: House of Peace

    444 aromatherapy way
  - ➢ Service(s): Reflexology massage, body mud wrap and facial
  - ➢ <u>Reflection: I left feeling so relaxed that I had to skip lunch and go home for a nap. I woke up feeling so fresh and new! My husband said I must have put special love into dinner because I was feeling so good lol I need more days like this.</u>

Use your bookmark to create lines if needed or write all over.

Do what you want on the week you want.

Do your best to focus on the Positive but journal **YOUR** truth on each item.

Please share with us on Instagram at @the52weekexperience

ENJOY!

NEVER LOSE YOURSELF AGAIN

- *Anything old can be new again.*

  Refurbish a piece of furniture around the home.

  - Date:

  - Item revamped or refurbished:

  - What did you do to upgrade item:

  - How long did the project take:

  - Reflection:

❖ **Have a seat at the table with the (relation)Ships... friend, business/career, romantic, parenting... Do you know what you want/need from others? What can you give/offer others? Your table may not have as many seated but focus on what you choose. Example:**

Type	Needed	Type	Given
Romantic/friends	Loyalty	Business	reliability
Business/romantic/friends	Reliability	parenting	Truth about life

➤ Date:

Type	**Given**

1.

2.

3.

4.

5.

6.

7.

8.

9.

10.

	Type	**Needed**
1.		
2.		
3.		
4.		
5.		
6.		
7.		
8.		
9.		
10.		

➢ Reflection:

- ❖ **Go Thrifting.**

  - ➢ Date:

  - ➢ Thrift Shops visited:

  - ➢ Best or any Good finds:

  - ➢ Reflection:

❖ *Try a new cuisine…* tear a sheet of paper into 8 pieces. Write different cuisine types. Cuisine examples- indian, cajun, greek, soul, thai, etc fold them and place into a bowl. Shake and pick one. Don't cheat yourself and ruin the experience. Ask around for suggestions or hit google to find a place to try for the cuisine selected.

➢ Date:

➢ Cuisine Selected:

➢ Restaurant/Carryout:

➢ What did you have:

➢ Reflection:

- ❖ ***Give Back.***

    Volunteer your time to a cause.

    - ➤ Date:

    - ➤ Charity/Cause selected:

    - ➤ Reason(s) for selecting Charity/Cause:

    - ➤ Service given to cause:

    - ➤ Reflection:

- ❖ *Have a Chic and Culture filled day*
  Get dressed up, have lunch and visit a Museum.

  - ➢ Date:

  - ➢ Museum:

  - ➢ Favorite Exhibit:

  - ➢ What did you wear:

  - ➢ Lunch:

  - ➢ Reflection:

- *Are you a true foodie?*

   Hit a food festival for the day.

   ➤ Date:

   ➤ Food Festival attended:

   ➤ What new foods did you try:

   ➤ Reflection:

- *Create your own special Valentine's Day.*
  Fall in Love with Self. Wear your best red fashions, treat self to a gift and hit a happy hour or mixer.

  - Date:

  - Gift purchased:

  - Happy Hour or Mixer Attended:

  - Meet at least one person- Who:

  - Reflection:

- ❖ *What food is your city or state known for?*
  Try out 3 of the top finds and YOU pick the best of the best!

  - ➢ Food your city or state is known for:

  - ➢ Three locations visited and when:

  - ➢ Winner and why:

  - ➢ Reflection:

- ❖ **Instead of a movie- Go to the theater for a play.**

    - ➢ Date:

    - ➢ Theater Visited:

    - ➢ Play seen:

    - ➢ If movie for play- which was better- the movie or play:

    - ➢ Reflection:

PEACE OF MIND IS THE BEST REWARD

- ❖ ***Learn from the pros***
  Attend a cooking class.

  - ➤ Date:

  - ➤ Location for class:

  - ➤ Dish(s) prepared:

  - ➤ Reflection:

- ❖ *YELL IT LOUD! BINGO!*

  Find your local Bingo Hall and go play.

  - ➢ Date:

  - ➢ Bingo hall:

  - ➢ How many cards played at once:

  - ➢ Prizes won:

  - ➢ Reflection:

- ❖ *Relax. Relate. Release…*

    Have a Spa day.

Tip: Bath houses offer multiple spa services, smoothies and healthy food options and relaxing areas.

- ➢ Date:

- ➢ Spa/Bath House Visited:

- ➢ Service(s):

- ➢ Reflection:

❖ *Go find where nature meets beauty…*
Visit a Botanical Garden or greenhouse.

➢ Date:

➢ Location visited:

➢ Favorite Flower/Exhibit:

➢ Reflection:

- ❖ *Channel Your inner Picasso*
  Go to a paint class.

  ➢ Date:

  ➢ Class location:

  ➢ Description of painting:

  ➢ Reflection:

- *Do you have to go all out for a good time?*
  Take the $30 Outing Challenge.

  - Date:

  - List details of how the $30 was spent. No cheating!

  - Reflection:

❖ *Feel Good Movie Marathon Night.*
   Movie Examples: Eat. Pray. Love., Sliding Doors, Waiting to Exhale, Claudine, Steel Magnolias, etc. Select what makes you feel good.

   ➢ Date:

   ➢ Movies:

   ➢ Start time: End time:

   ➢ Snacks/Menu:

   ➢ Reflection:

LOVE SELF

- ❖ **Grab a blanket or chair and catch a movie in the park.**

    - ➢ Date:

    - ➢ Park:

    - ➢ Movie:

    - ➢ Reflection:

- ❖ *Like Live Music?*

    See a Jazz band at a nice bar or lounge.

    - ➢ Date:

    - ➢ Location:

    - ➢ Favorite Number played by band:

    - ➢ Meet at least one new person- Who:

    - ➢ Reflection:

❖ *Can you see the bigger picture?*

Put together a puzzle. Minimum of 500 pieces.

Tip: Perfect for a rainy or snow day in. finished item can be hung in your home!

➢ Date:

➢ Describe the puzzle picture:

➢ Piece Count:

➢ Completion time:

➢ Reflection:

- ❖ *Good Health is Wealth.*

  Take 30, 60 or 90 days to reach your health/fitness goal(s)

  ➤ Start Date:

  ➤ Goal(s):

  ➤ Plan to reach goal:

  ➤ End Date:

  ➤ Reflection:

NO.

IT'S A COMPLETE SENTENCE. NO EXPLAINING NEEDED

- ❖ *You could never be to safe!*
  Take a self defense class.

  - ➢ Date:

  - ➢ Location of class:

  - ➢ Defenses learned:

  - ➢ Reflection:

- ❖ *Work it out!*
  Attend a workout class.

  - ➢ Date:

  - ➢ Location of class:

  - ➢ Type of class:

  - ➢ Class length:

  - ➢ Reflection:

- *Keep it sexy… for you.*

  Treat yourself to a sexy boudoir photo shoot.

  - Date:

  - Photographer:

  - Theme:

  - What did you wear:

  - Reflection:

- ❖ ***SHOW ME SOME MOVES!***
  Take a dance class.

  - ➢ Date:

  - ➢ Location for class:

  - ➢ Type of Dance:

  - ➢ Reflection:

❖ *Shake things up.*

Treat yourself to a makeover.

Tip: Try a bold lipstick and/or A new hair color or style completely outside of your norm.

➢ Date:

➢ New look(s) tried:

➢ Reflection:

❖ *Get to know a few new faces…*
   Join Meetup.com and connect with a group for your interest.

   ➢ Date:

   ➢ Group(s) Joined:

   ➢ First Outing Details:

   ➢ Reflection:

- ❖ **Join a book club or read a new book on your own. Any kind. Pick one. Finish within the month.**

  - ➢ Date:

  - ➢ Book Selected:

  - ➢ Type and description:

  - ➢ Instant Reflection:

  - ➢ Reflection at the end of reading:

- ❖ *Learn a new craft.*
  There are tons to choose from.
  Knitting. Sewing. Etc What are you choosing?

  ➢ Date:

  ➢ Craft Selected:

  ➢ Class location:

  ➢ Instant Reflection:

  ➢ Reflection at the end of learning craft:

❖ *It's nice to know where you are heading.*
  Create a vision board.

Tip: Hang it where you will see it each day.

- Date:

- 5 top items on your board:

- Plans to complete/reach goals:

- Reflection:

- *Shopping scavenger hunt.*

    Tear 5 pieces of paper. Write down 5 colors outside of black. Fold and put in bowl. Shake and pick. For the color chosen- go on the hunt for a dress or pants and top, shoes, and purse or jacket in the color selected.

Tip: Doesn't have to be an outfit but must find at least 3 fashion pieces. No cheating or online shopping! It's a fun way to add color to your closet.

- Date:

- Color Selected:

- Items Purchased:

- Reflection:

IT'S NOT SELFFISH TO CARE FOR SELF

- ❖ Want to build better habits? Start a goal jar. Here's how it works: Find large jar or box with lid. Cut money slot. List habits you want to build with amount of money you will deposit for each task you complete daily. Ex. 1hr of reading $2 Exercise $1 No sugar $3 Each day deposit the amount for habits completed. At the end of your chosen date, count your reward and treat yourself for a job well done!

  - ➢ Date started/ended:

  - ➢ Positive habits to create (ex. pack lunch, exercise, drinking more water, reducing tv/social media, reading more, etc):

  - ➢ How much will each task reward:

  - ➢ Total Reward Saved:

  - ➢ What was done with reward:

  - ➢ Reflection of activity:

❖ **Plan and Prepare a dinner party for you and your closet friends. Add more fun by providing props or by asking all to dress to match the theme of dinner. Example: if serving Mexican ask guest to dress with sombreros, colorful ponchos and more.**

➢ Date:

➢ Guest List:

➢ Theme:

➢ Menu:

➢ Reflection:

- ❖ *Thankful for certain people in your life?*

  Set a budget per gift. (ex. $10 per) Be creative. Wrap and personally surprise them with the special delivery.

  ➢ Date:

  ➢ Gifts for who:

  ➢ Gifts made or purchased:

  ➢ Reflection:

- ❖ **Attend a seminar and learn something. Empowerment. Relationship. Home Buying. Religion. There are so many to choose from.**

  - ➢ Date:

  - ➢ Type of Seminar:

  - ➢ Reason for selecting seminar:

  - ➢ Location:

  - ➢ Hosted by:

  - ➢ Reflection:

- ❖ ***PURGE DAY!!!***

  Clean your closets and home of anything that no longer serves purpose… or works.

  - ➤ Date:

  - ➤ Items tossed:

  - ➤ Time Started: Time Ended:

  - ➤ Reflection:

- ❖ *Release. Relax. Reflect.*

  Light candles, make a pot of tea and write… Write a letter to your younger self. Cover the good, the bad and ugly. Forgive her. Get it all down. Write one to the woman you are today. Encourage her. Let her know where you are about to go with your future. Move forward.

  - ➤ Date:

  - ➤ What are you doing with letters and why:

  - ➤ Reflection:

❖ *Run away from home!*
Check for flight sales and getaway for a few days. Las Vegas, New York and South Beach are good places one can travel alone and have a safe good time.

- Dates:

- Place visited:

- Favorite place visited or activity done while away:

- Meet at least one new person. Who was it:

- Reflection:

- *No. no. NO! take a day.*

    One full day and tell everyone NO! Have a selfish day to put everything and everyone on the NO list. It will be so refreshing to have put you first.

    ➢ Date:

    ➢ What kinds of things did you refuse today that you would have normally agreed to?

    ➢ Reflection:

- ❖ *Learn to love or Love self more…*
  Go adult toy and lingerie shopping.

  ➢ Date:

  ➢ Type of items purchased:

  ➢ Reflection:

❖ *Life breeds Life.*

Plant something. Favorite flower, house plants, herbs, veggies or fruit. Plant something and watch it grow over time.

➢ Date:

➢ Type of Seed(s) Planted:

➢ Instant Reflection:

➢ 3 month Reflection:

REFUEL
FOR YOU

- *Make grandma proud!*

  Create a new or improved upon a cookie recipe… FROM SCRATCH!

  - Date:

  - Type of cookies:

  - Reflection:

- ❖ **Leben (German), Vivere (Italian), Vivre (French), Vivir (Spanish), Hayi (Arabic), Salgo Issda (Korean), Zhit (Russian)… no matter what language you say it in- LIVE! Learn a new language.**

    - ➢ Dates:

    - ➢ Language Selected:

    - ➢ Reason for selecting this language:

    - ➢ Reflection:

- ❖ ***Brunch and Binge.***

  Make your favorite breakfast and lunch items then watch all the seasons of a trending show.

  - ➢ Date:

  - ➢ Menu:

  - ➢ Show(s) selected:

  - ➢ Reflection:

- **Visit your local farmers market.**

  - Date:

  - Market visited and Location:

  - Weather during visit:

  - Deals found or items purchased:

  - Reflection:

- **Complete a photography challenge. Check out google for one that works for you. Which challenge? How many days does it last?**

  - Dates:

  - Challenged Selected:

  - Instant Reflection:

  - Reflection at end of challenge:

❖ *You could never learn enough.*
   Find and take FREE online course.

   ➢ Date:

   ➢ Type of course:

   ➢ Reason for selecting course:

   ➢ Instant Reflection:

   ➢ Reflection at end of course:

❖ *Learn about your roots and build your family tree.*
   Complete an ancestry.com or 23andme.com profile

   ➢ Date:

   ➢ Family Origin:

   ➢ Most interesting thing learned about your origin:

   ➢ Reflection:

- ❖ *What are you willing to sacrifice for your goal*s?
  Set a financial goal with date and create a plan to achieve it.

  ➢ Date Started: Achievement Date:

  ➢ Financial Goal:

  ➢ Plan to reach goal:

  ➢ Instant Reflection:

  ➢ Reflection on achievement date:

❖ *See a man about a horse.* 🐴

Take a horse riding lesson. If you are familiar with riding- go on a trail ride instead.

➢ Date:

➢ Farm visited:

➢ Breed of horse:

➢ Reflection:

- ❖ **Go out for karaoke and be bold enough to get up to sing** 🎤

  - ➢ Date:

  - ➢ Location for karaoke:

  - ➢ What song did you choose or best song selected:

  - ➢ Reflection:

- ***YOU BETTER WERK!!!***
  Attend a Drag show.

  - Date:

  - Brunch Attended:

  - Favorite Performer:

  - Reflection:

LIFE IS BEAUTIFUL AND SO ARE YOU

BONUS AREA FOR YOU TO CREATE AN ACTIVITY OF YOUR OWN:

- **Activity:**

  - Date:

  - Highlight of outing:

BONUS AREA FOR YOU TO CREATE AN ACTIVITY OF YOUR OWN:

- **Activity:**

  - Date:

  - Highlight of outing:

BONUS AREA FOR YOU TO CREATE AN ACTIVITY OF YOUR OWN:

- ❖ **Activity:**

  - ➤ Date:

  - ➤ Highlight of outing:

Overall Reflection…

On our final pages is where you reflect on your overall experiences. From the start, halfway completed point and once the journal is full. Note your general honest feel and view on the time taken for YOU.

Date:

Top 5 items you will complete first:

Beginning Reflection:

Continued

Overall Reflection...

Take a peek back at your beginning reflection AFTER you complete this one to see if any changes on how you think of and have been taking time for you.

Date:

Favorite item completed so far:

Top 5 items you are excited about completing next:

Mid-Point Reflection:

Continued

Overall Reflection...

Take a peek back at your last reflections AFTER you complete this one to see if any changes if how you think of and have been taking time for you.

Date:

Favorite items completed:

Final Reflection:

Thank you for your support.

Be sure to check out our other series in the 52 Week Experience.

Follow and share with us on IG @the52weekexperience

www.ingramcontent.com/pod-product-compliance
Lightning Source LLC
Chambersburg PA
CBHW071032080526
44587CB00015B/2588